What Was the Wicked Witch's Real Name?
and Other Character Riddles

Joanne E. Bernstein and Paul Cohen

pictures by Ann Iosa

Albert Whitman & Company, Niles, Illinois

Also by Joanne E. Bernstein and Paul Cohen
Happy Holiday Riddles to You!
More Unidentified Flying Riddles
Un-Frog-Gettable Riddles
Unidentified Flying Riddles

Library of Congress Cataloging in Publication Data

Bernstein, Joanne E.
    What was the wicked witch's real name?

    Summary: Includes more than 130 humorous riddles
involving a variety of familiar characters from the
Bible, fairy tales, nursery rhymes, comic strips, songs,
TV cartoons, and well-known books.
    1. Riddles, Juvenile. 2. Characters and
characteristics—Juvenile humor. [1. Riddles.
2. Wit and humor] I. Cohen, Paul, 1945-
II. Iosa, Ann, ill. III. Title.
PN6371.5.B44   1986   818'.5402   86-1648
ISBN 0-8075-8854-7

The text of this book is printed in fourteen-point Frutiger.

Text © 1986 by Joanne E. Bernstein and Paul Cohen
Illustrations © 1986 by Ann Iosa
Published in 1986 by Albert Whitman & Company, Niles, Illinois
Published simultaneously in Canada
by General Publishing, Limited, Toronto

Once U-pun a Time

What did Snow White sing while waiting for her
 photos?
"Some day my prints will come."

What business was Cinderella's husband in?
Toilet paper. He was Prince Charmin'.

What did he say when she hugged him?
"Please don't squeeze the Charmin'."

When did the handsome prince get conked by a
 rabbit?
After he said, "Rapunzel, let down your hare."

Who barked the Three Little Pigs' house down?
The Big Bad Woof.

Which fairy tale takes place in a bakery?
Beauty and the Yeast.

Who was Sleeping Beauty's sad sister?
Weeping Beauty.

Who was her maid?
Sweeping Beauty.

Why did the princess's feet fall asleep?
She was wearing sleeping booties.

How did Cinderella break her leg?
She fell off her wicked stepladder.

What did Gretel say when her stepmother
   left her in the forest?
"Look Hans, no Ma."

Which vegetables chat with Jack?
Jack and the beans talk.

Take a Gander at Mother Goose

Who made a loud noise when he met the pieman?
Cymbal Simon.

What would you get if Bo Peep married Uncle
Scrooge?
Bo Cheap.

Who cures mouse-infested clocks?
The Hickory Dickory Doc.

Who had so many carrots she didn't know what to do?
The old woman who lived in a stew.

Which stew ingredient did she like least?
The ugly dumpling.

Who called for his pipe, his bowl, and his six-pack
 of soda?
Old King Cola.

Who was Humpty Dumpty?
A camel who threw off all his riders.

Which character couldn't catch a baseball?
Little Miss Muff-it.

What should you do with a Mother Goose book?
Take a gander, of course.

Oz and Ends

What was the Wicked Witch's real name?
Ted. You know, "Ting, tong, the witch is Ted."

What football position did she play?
Left cackle.

Which mouse led Dorothy to Oz?
The yellow brick rodent.

What did people in the Emerald City call their
dinosaur?
The Lizard of Oz.

Literary Lunacy

What is Jules Verne's famous story about a
   plumber?
20,000 Leaks Under the Sink.

What Dickens character liked pretzels?
Oliver Twist.

What man from Vulcan sailed on the *Nautilus?*
Captain Nimoy.

What Hans Christian Andersen character always
   falls on her face?
Stumbelina.

Who is the oiliest character in all literature?
The Count of Monte Crisco.

What did Tuck say when the Sheriff of Nottingham
  put him in oil?
"You can't boil me! I'm a friar."

Why were the Three Musketeers so fat?
It was always lunge time.

Did Hucklebewwy Finn twavel by boat?
No, by Twain.

What did Aladdin rub unsuccessfully?
Aladdin's Lump.

What did Robinson Crusoe say when he discovered
 the footprints?
"Thank goodness it's Friday!"

Which monkey got mad at the man with the yellow
 hat?
Furious George.

Who writes nonsense cookbooks for kids?
Dr. Sauce.

Why do children keep reading *Lord of the Rings*?
They get in the Hobbit.

Peter Pandemonium

Which fairy smelled bad?
Stinkerbell.

Why did the airplane fly past Peter Pan's house?
The pilot saw the "Never Land" sign.

Which pirate stayed home from school?
Captain Hookey.

Why did his sword have a hole in the middle?
It was a life saber.

Why did Captain Hook pick up the phone?
He thought he heard a croc-o-dial.

Stupid Heroes

Who leaps into tall buildings with a single bound?
Stupid Man.

Who is the least successful superheroine?
Blunder Woman.

What two vegetables are round, red, and fight crime?
Beetman and Radish.

Who is the most obnoxious superhero?
Bratman.

What is Superman's toughest job?
Remembering which phone booth he left his pants in.

Why did Superman leave his planet in the evening?
He was afraid of the Krypton-nite.

Why does Superman's girlfriend love puns?
Because they're the Lois form of humor.

Which superhero lives on potatoes?
Spud-erman.

Why couldn't Batman go fishing?
Because Robin ate the worms.

Which He-Man character is hardest to hear?
Mur-mur Man.

Which owns the most shoes?
Man-E-Laces.

Which superhero always feels blue?
Aqua Man.

Tel-a-Riddle

Who stinks up the classroom?
Pépé le Pupil.

Who hops away from Wile E. Coyote?
The Toad Runner.

What did Wile E. Coyote have for dinner?
The Road Walker.

How does Yogi Bear furnish his den?
With the bear essentials.

What do you call a rabbit owned by a mosquito?
A bug's bunny.

What makes things go wrong in Smurfdom?
Smurfy's Law.

What does Bam Bam make in his diapers?
Yabba-dabba-doo-doo.

How did Sylvester's war end?
With a Tweety.

What did Bullwinkle call his fan club?
The Moose-keteers.

Toying Around

What do you call a miniature Cabbage Patch doll?
A Brussels sprout.

Why do they make a lot of Cabbage Patch dolls?
To make a lot of Cabbage Patch dollars.

Which Cabbage Patch dolls are most expensive?
Those bought at a preemie-um.

What are the most overpriced pickles?
Cabbage Patch dills.

Can you smash Cabbage Patch dolls?
No, but you can Pound Puppies.

What do GoBots do after six days of work?
Go Rust.

Who won't let go of her noonday meal?
Hugga Lunch.

What does the Jolly Green Giant do down in the valley?
Hoe, hoe, hoe.

Who is Mr. Clean's identical twin?
Mr. Clone.

What food does Heidi's dog prefer?
Alp-o.

What is Tony the Tiger's favorite flavor?
G-r-r-r-a-a-a-pe!

What would you get if Pete Rose married Betty Crocker?
A better batter.

Noah Good Riddle?

Who was the fastest runner in history?
Adam. He was first in the human race.

Who was the first man mentioned in the Bible?
Chap. 1.

At what time was Adam created?
Just before Eve.

Who killed a quarter of the world's population?
Cain, when he killed Abel.

What did Noah say when all the animals were aboard?
"Now I herd everything."

Was there any money on the ark?
Yes. The ducks took bills, the frogs took green backs, and the skunks took scents.

Why was there no card-playing on the ark?
Noah stood on the deck.

Why was it hard for Noah to catch fish?
He had only two worms.

What was Noah's profession?
He was an arch-itect.

Who was the straightest man in the Bible?
Joseph. Pharaoh made him a ruler.

Was David sure he could beat Goliath?
No, but he took a shot at it.

Who was the most popular actor in the Bible?
Samson. He brought the house down.

Where was Solomon's temple?
On the side of his head.

How did Jonah feel when the whale swallowed
    him?
Down in the mouth.

What was left after the spider sampled apple juice?
Just eensy-weensy cider.

Did you hear the song about the woman who ate a
   potato?
Sure. "There was an old lady who swallowed a
   fry."

What song is about pickle-making?
The Farmer in the Dill. (It's cucumbersome work.)

Who has a farm and has made billions of hamburgers?
Old McDonald's.

Why did Jiminy Cricket get lost in the forest?
He let his conscience be his guide.

Zoo-Illogical Riddles

Which horse had the worst breath?
The Black Scallion.

Which lumberjack rode him?
Paul Onion.

What do you feed Fat Albert's horse?
Hay, hay, hay.

Why did the pig cry over Chicken Little's message?
He thought she said the *sty* was falling.

Whose flute-playing drove all the snakes out of
    Hamelin?
The Pied Viper.

Which chicken didn't cross the road?
Chicken Middle.

Which bear never grew up?
Peter Panda.

Who was Winnie the Pooh's identical brother?
Twinnie the Pooh.

Who puts you to sleep in the campground?
Smokey the Bore.

How did Thumper's story end?
Hoppily ever after.

Westward Ho Ho

Which Indian had the smallest laugh?
Minne-ha-ha.

Who did she marry?
He-he-he-Man.

How did Hiawatha?
With thoap and water.

Who was the slowest Indian maiden?
Pokey-hontas.

Who lent money in the Old West?
The Loan Arranger.

What did the Loan Arranger call money from
  Cleveland?
O-hi-o Silver!

How does a restaurant charge for bison steaks?
With a buffalo bill.

Which Western heroes were loudest at dinner?
Wild Bill Hiccup and Wyatt Burp.

Criminal Activity

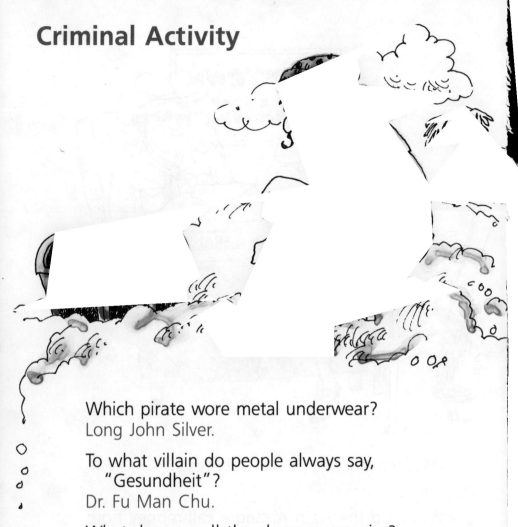

Which pirate wore metal underwear?
Long John Silver.

To what villain do people always say,
   "Gesundheit"?
Dr. Fu Man Chu.

What do you call the cheaper vampire?
Discount Dracula.

How did the He-Man villain get into the Grayskull
   Castle?
He used his Skeletor key.

Which villain never speaks?
Shyman Legree.

What famous sleuth is an artist?
Nancy Drew.

Who is a timid detective?
Harriet the Shy.

Who are the strongest detectives?
The Hardy boys.

Do adults read stories about boy detectives?
Hardy ever.

Where do retired detectives live?
The Sherlock Homes.

What did Holmes call the canal that carries
    food to the stomach?
Alimentary, my dear Watson.

Funnies from the Funnies

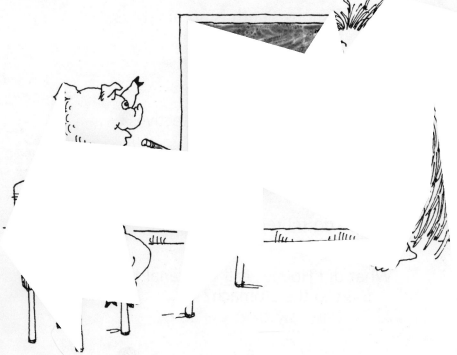

Who was Porky Pig's sharper cousin?
Porky Pine. Get the point?

What does Donald Duck call his jokes?
Wisequacks.

What do Huey, Dewey, and Louie say about them?
Phooey.

Who was Donald's ancestor in Sherwood Forest?
Fryer Duck.

What's green and walks through walls?
Casper the Friendly Grape.

Who was Charlie Brown's cowardly cousin?
Charlie Yellow.

Who was Charlie Brown's worn-out dog?
Droopy.

Who ripped up all of Beethoven's music?
Shredder.

Who was Orphan Annie's poorer uncle?
Daddy Four-Bucks.

What has antlers and eats cheese?
Mickey Moose.

Jokes About Folks

Who ran the first night school?
King Arthur.

Which knight was always out of breath?
Sir Pants-a-lot.

Which knight wouldn't stop mambo-ing?
Sir Dance-a-lot. (If you don't know what a mambo
is, ask your mam-bo.)

Which famous patriot was a vegetable?
Uncle Yam.

What do Alexander the Great and Smokey the Bear
have in common?
The same middle name.

How should a character riddle book end?
Happily ever laughter.